W9-AOJ-862

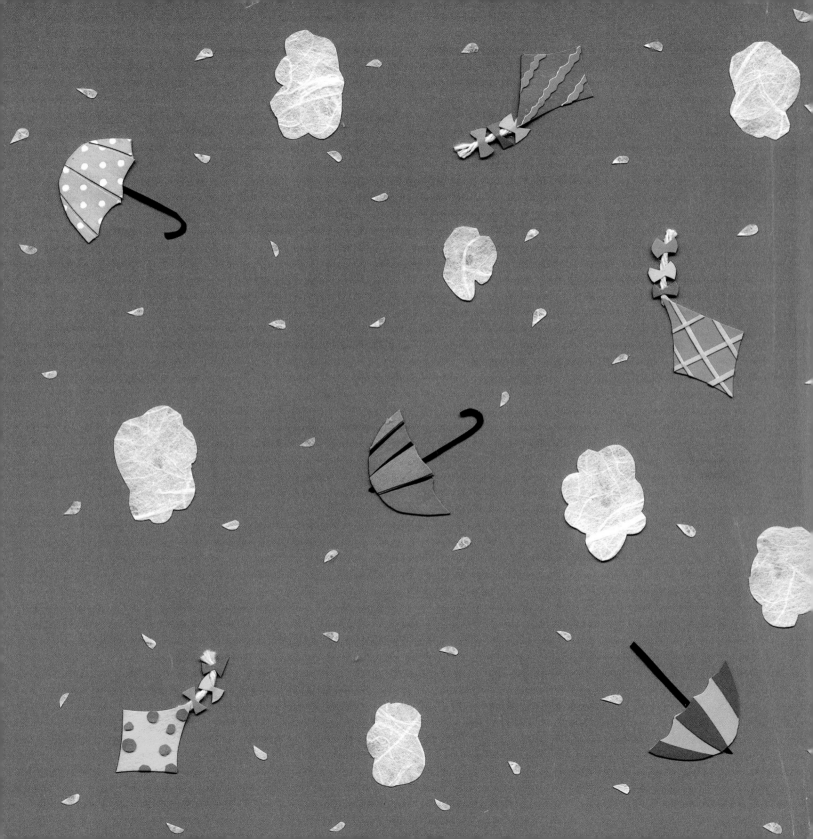

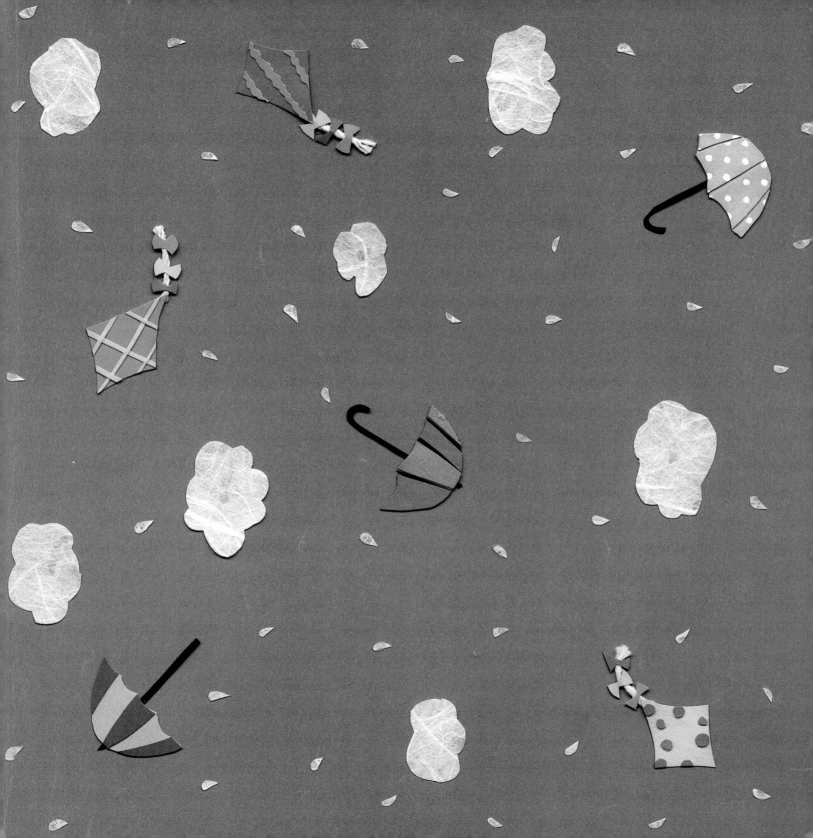

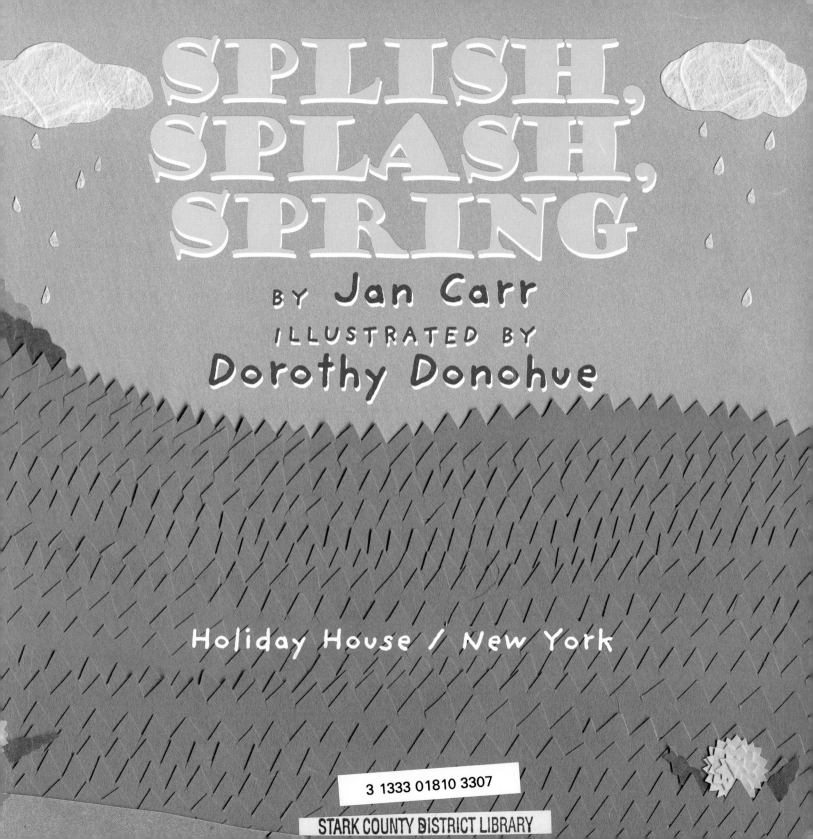

SPLISH, SPLASH, SPRING

BY **Jan Carr**

ILLUSTRATED BY

Dorothy Donohue

Holiday House / New York

Text copyright © 2001 by Jan Carr
Illustrations copyright © 2001 by Dorothy Donohue
All Rights Reserved
Printed in the United States of America
www.holidayhouse.com
The text typeface is Providence.
The collage artwork was created with cut paper.
First Edition

Library of Congress Cataloging-in-Publication Data
Carr, Jan.
Splish, splash, spring / by Jan Carr; illustrated by Dorothy Donohue.—1st ed.
p. cm.
Summary: Illustrations and rhyming text describe some
of the delights of spring.
ISBN 0-8234-1578-3 (hardcover)
[1. Spring—Fiction. 2. Stories in rhyme.]
I. Donohue, Dorothy, ill. II. Title.

PZ8.3.C21687 Sp 2001
[E]
00-039605

To Charlie and Jessie,
the new buds on our family tree,
and to Granny Janny, spring chicken
—J. C.

For James,
I picked spring—
just for you
—D. D.

Spring is sloppy
So raindroppy!
Stomp in puddles
Splash about

Sun comes peeking
Hide-and-seeking
Days are playful
Spring's a-sprout!

Chit-chit-cheeping
Who's that peeping?
Baby robins
Beg for bugs

Better dig one
Get a big one!
Grub up earthworms
Slimy slugs

Hocus-pocus!
There's a crocus!

Plucky petals
Brave the chill

Frilly, silly
Daffodilly
Willy-nilly
Down the hill

Kites are swooping
Loop-de-looping
Snapping, flapping
Look at me!

Wind comes whipping
Grip is slipping
Tangle, dangle
Up a tree

Boughs are bloomy
So perfumy!
Thunder threatens
Skip-skidoo!

Race the raindrops
Windowpane drops
I picked posies—

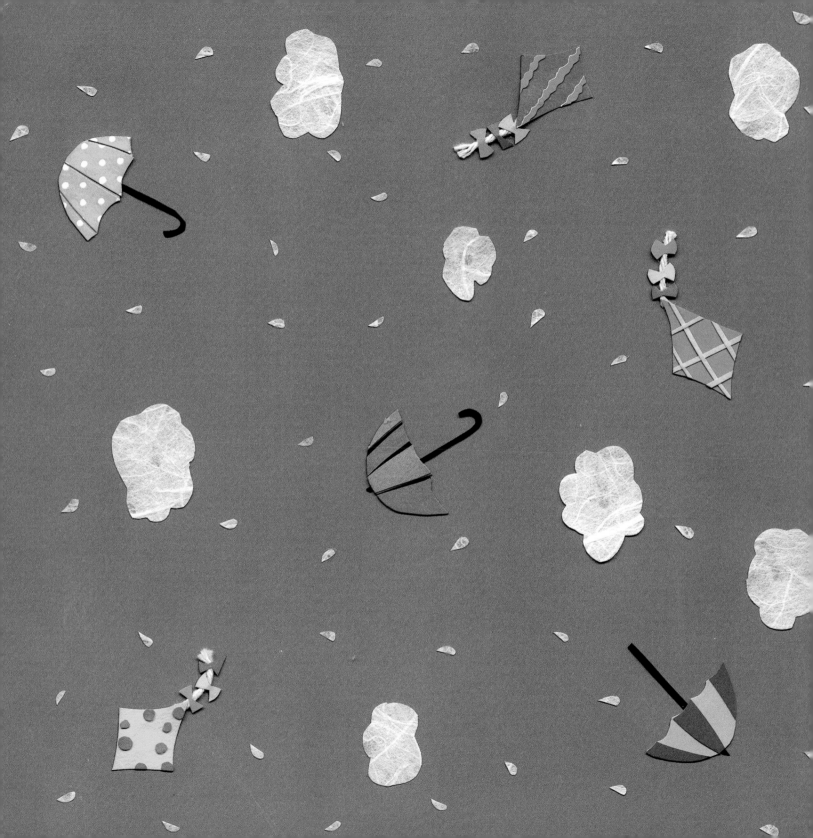

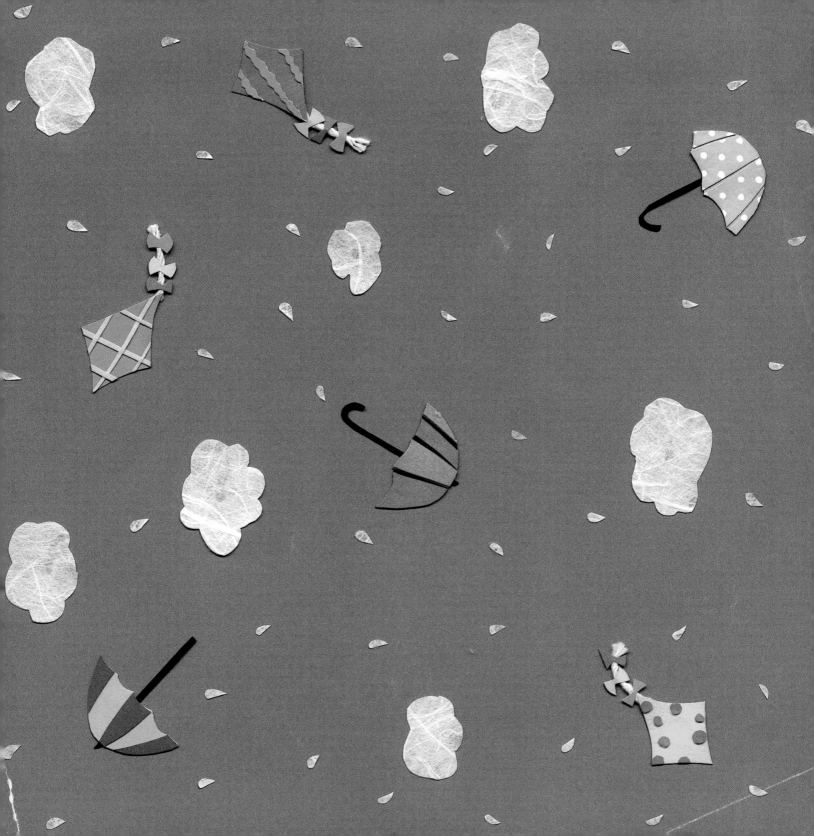